I STILL CAN'T BREATHE 400 YEARS LATER

Testimony and Guide to Overcoming Adversity

Written by
Lewis Burt

This book may be purchased in bulk for educational, business, or sales promotional use.

© 2022 by Words of Wisdom Publishing.
Published in Pittsburg, PA.
Book Design by Chamika Dinesh of Sri Lanka.
Illustrated by Ashley Mae Pancho.

ISBN (Paperback): 979-8-9857424-0-4
ISBN (Ebook): 979-8-9857424-1-1
Library of Congress Control Number (LCCN): 2022902389

Follow Lewis Burt on social media:

Twitter: @RealMrBurt
Instagram: @RealMrBurt
Facebook: @RealMrBurt

CONTENT

Dedication...1

Acknowledgments.......................................2

About the Author 3

Preface 4

Introduction 5

Stephon Clark 6

Freddy Gray 8

Eric Garner 10

Tamir Rice 12

Antwon Rose 14

Akai Gurley 16

Philando Castile.......................................18

Brianna Taylor...20

Emmett Till 22

Medgar Evers 24

Rosa Parks 26

Million Man March....................................28

Kunta Kinte 30

Harriet Tubman..32

Martin Luther King Jr. 34

Epilogue...36

Dedication

THIS BOOK IS dedicated to everyone who has experienced, is currently experiencing, or will experience some form of adversity in their lifetime.

Remember that you are resilient; your life has value and purpose, regardless of what you may be going through at the moment.

Please keep the faith, remain hopeful, and remember that you are loved.

ACKNOWLEDGMENTS

TO GOD, MY LORD AND SAVIOR: thank you for using me as a vessel to help bring more hope, healing, positivity, and love into the world.

To any and everyone who has fallen victim to police brutality, racism, and hate: your pain is my pain.

ABOUT THE AUTHOR

BORN AND RAISED in Pittsburgh, Pennsylvania, Lewis Burt believes in humanity and equal rights for everyone. *I Still Can't Breathe 400 Years Later* is a mirror into his heart, reflecting love, defeat, pain, maturity, and hope.

PREFACE

THIS BOOK IS about the permanent scars left on the hearts of millions from police brutality, racism, and hate.

> *Psalms 34:4-5 | I sought the Lord, and he delivered me from all my fears. Those whose look to him are radiant; their faces are never covered with shame.*

INTRODUCTION

I'LL NEVER FORGET May 5th of 2014. On that day a plainclothes police officer tased me, handcuffed me, beat me, put his knee on my neck, and whispered in my ear saying, "killing you would've been awesome." I still wake up in cold sweats and can't seem to shake the honesty and hatred I heard in the cop's voice that day.

That cop told me I was lucky to be alive because he should have killed me. That officer's comments made me feel worthless, terrified, and grateful all at the same time.

I hope and pray for change because I don't want to spend the rest of my life worrying about dying in something as simple as a traffic stop.

I still can't breathe, 400 years later.

> *Proverbs 6:16-19 | There are six things that the Lord hates, seven that are detestable to him: haughty eyes, a lying tongue, hands that shed innocent blood, a heart that devises wicked schemes, feet that are quick to rush into evil, a false witness who pours out lies, and a person who stirs up conflict in the community.*

STEPHON CLARK

EVERY TIME I was at my grandmother's house, I felt peaceful and safe.

It was like heaven on earth; that was my favorite place. The place where I could go to feel loved, and the place where I could breathe and feel free.

I never thought that my grandmother's backyard would turn into a cemetery. I never thought that at twenty-two years of age, God would call me home.

I definitely didn't think I'd get shot at more than twenty times for holding a mobile phone. I never thought I'd get killed from raining gunfire from the police.

Now I'm a statistic of police brutality and the deceased.

Now that I'm gone, will things ever change? Will justice ever prevail, or will things remain the same?

Will a time come when we can witness equal justice under the sun? I was killed by police, but no charges were filed because my phone could've been a gun.

YEAR | 2018

WHAT HE WAS DOING | Standing in his grandmother's backyard.

HOW HE WAS KILLED | Officers said they believed Clark was holding a gun as they shot at him more than twenty times. Clark was only holding a mobile phone.

ACTION TAKEN | The district attorney declined to file criminal charges. Clark's family reached a $2.4M settlement with the city of Sacramento.

We still can't breathe
A knee is on our necks
Life left
92%
Food for the soul

Stand for something or fall for anything.

Exodus 20:13 | Thou shalt not kill.

FREDDY GRAY

I'M SURROUNDED BY four walls, but I'm not trapped in a cell.
My hands and my feet are shackled, and I'm being forced to joy ride through hell.

The flames are intense, and I feel like my spine is severed.
My chances of survival are short, and I mean that by all measures.

The cops are against me, and right now my life is in their hands.
I don't have a seatbelt on, so I am surviving. I don't think that's in their plans.

My lifeless body lay stiff for over forty-five minutes.
There were six officers who played a part in my death, and now my life is finished.

Police brutality is a death sentence, and this is not the life I chose.
This life chose me because I'm Black, and now the truth is exposed.

Black males are targets and police kill us for no reason.
That's a lie. The reason is because racist cops view Blacks as game, and it's always hunting season.

YEAR | 2015

WHAT HE WAS DOING | Sitting in a police van.

HOW HE WAS KILLED | Gray had been arrested and placed in a police van. He was found dead forty-five minutes later with his spinal cord nearly severed. His hands and feet had been shackled, and without a seatbelt he could not protect himself as he was tossed around inside the vehicle.

ACTION TAKEN | Six officers were charged in connection with Gray's death. Three were acquitted, and three had their cases dropped. The city reached a $6.4M settlement with Gray's family.

We still can't breathe
A knee is on our necks
Life left
87%
Food for the soul

Stand together or fight alone.

Romans 13:10 | Love does no harm to a neighbor; therefore, love is the fulfillment of the law.

Eric Garner

I'M A FATHER of six and I say that proudly.
I'll work a nine-to-five or sell loose cigarettes to provide for my family, and I'll scream that loudly!

A father's job is to provide, protect, and to be that rock.
That's all I was trying to do: provide for my children, and then here comes the cops.

Judge, jury, and executioner have a chokehold around my neck.
Eleven times I was able to gasp the words, "I can't breathe!" but the cops still showed me no respect.

Now my vision is going blurry, and everything is going dark.
I'm praying to God that my death won't be in vain, and that my name will start a spark.

The spark that will open the eyes of millions to witness the Black man's everyday reality.
I won't forget to mention that Black men and Black women are being slaughtered by the hands of police brutality.

YEAR | 2014

WHAT HE WAS DOING | Allegedly selling loose cigarettes.

HOW HE WAS KILLED | An officer held Eric in a chokehold that he did not release, in spite of Garner saying, "I can't breathe!" eleven times.

ACTION TAKEN | A grand jury declined to indict the officer who used deadly force. He was placed on desk duty after the incident. He was fired in 2009. The city reached a settlement with the Garner family for $5.9M.

We still can't breathe
A knee is on our necks
Life left
81%
Food for the soul

Know your worth.

> *Matthew 27:4 | Saying, "I have sinned by betraying innocent blood." And they said, "What is that to us? You see to it!"*

TAMIR RICE

MY CURFEW IS when the streetlights come on, and I have to be in before dark.
One of my favorite things to do is to play in the park.

I love games, sports, and I like to play cops and robbers.
I never thought that playing in the park at twelve years old would become a problem.

That's because I'm a child, and I thought I could live carefree.
Not here in America! Being young and Black with a toy gun spells R-I-P.

Where can I play? Where can I go?
Will the police ever stop bullying us? How will we know?

I was twelve years old with a lot of dreams.
I was so excited to turn thirteen.

A cop killed me for playing with my toy gun.
A cop killed me, and I was just a kid having fun.

YEAR | 2014

WHAT HE WAS DOING | Playing with a toy gun in the park.

HOW HE WAS KILLED | Within two seconds of arriving at the park, an officer fatally shot Rice. Police then tackled his fourteen-year-old sister to the ground, handcuffed her, and put her in the back of a police car. It took four minutes for officers to administer first aid to Rice. He died in the hospital the following day.

ACTION TAKEN | No officers were indicted. One officer received a ten-day suspension. The city of Cleveland agreed to pay Rice's family $6M to settle a civil lawsuit.

We still can't breathe
A knee is on our necks
Life left
74%
Food for the soul

Choose love over hate; have compassion and empathy for others.

> *Matthew 5:4 | Blessed are those who mourn for they shall be comforted.*

Antwon Rose

I HAD A dream to be eighteen.
My dream was shattered when I was murdered at seventeen.

The cops pulled us over, and I started fleeing from the scene.
I was fleeing because I feared for my life, and I'd seen too many things.

I'd heard countless stories of cops killing unarmed Black men for no reason.
Now I have three bullet holes in my body, and it's hard to keep breathing.

Is this cycle really repeating? I'm only seventeen.
I had my whole life ahead of me! I had big dreams!

Now my life is over for being in the wrong place at the wrong time.
If the car you're in matches a police description, that can be the reason that you die.

I had a dream to be eighteen.
My dream was shattered when a cop killed me at seventeen.

YEAR | 2018

WHAT HE WAS DOING | Riding in the car as a passenger.

HOW HE WAS KILLED | Fled during a traffic stop. Rose was shot three times while unarmed.

ACTION TAKEN | Homicide charges were filed against the officers accused. The officer was acquitted on all charges.

We still can't breathe
A knee is on our necks
Life left
70%
Food for the soul

Stop Black on Black violence!

Proverbs 17:15 | He who justifies the wicked, and he who condemns the just, both them alike are an abomination to the Lord.

Akai Gurley

I NEVER THOUGHT that I'd get shot and killed by a cop just for walking out my front door.
Bullets penetrating through my flesh...open your eyes! This is not a silent war.

This is police brutality at its core.
Police treat Blacks like we're nothing, but we're more.

Innocent blood spilled in the hallway on the project floor.
I don't think I'm going to make it, and that's a sign I can't ignore.

What did the cops even shoot me for?
I guess they were thinking, "that'll be one less more."

I bet there will be no justice, and the cop who killed me will get a slap on the wrist for this.
The justice system favors the blue shield, and racism controls it.

Manslaughter for shooting and killing me, you'd think that would carry jail time?
I lost my life from the hands of that cop, but community service and probation is just fine?

YEAR | 2014

WHAT HE WAS DOING | Walking down the stairs in the building where he lived.

HOW HE WAS KILLED | Two officers were conducting a "vertical patrol" in a housing project. One of the officers entered an unlit stairwell and fired his weapon. The bullet bounced off the wall and killed Gurley.

ACTION TAKEN | The officer was fired. He was convicted of manslaughter and official misconduct in 2016. He was sentenced to five years' probation and community service.

We still can't breathe
A knee is on our necks
Life left
63%
Food for the soul

Uplift your brothers and sisters. Become an inspiration.

John 7:24 | Stop judging by mere appearances, but instead judge correctly.

PHILANDO CASTILE

I'M A FATHER who was pulled over in a traffic stop with his girlfriend and his daughter.
I calmly warned the officer about my legal firearm before I was slaughtered.

It was as if that cop didn't even consider my life for a second, and that made me feel worthless.
That cop ordered me to reach for my driver's license, and then he shot me on purpose.

My daughter was in the car watching me bleed out, and now she's permanently scarred.
My girlfriend went live on Facebook, hoping for a charge.

Charges that would bring justice for these five bullet holes in my body.
Justice because I abided by the law...and the police still shot me.

At that moment, my life was in that officer's hands, and he didn't respect me.
He chose to kill by shooting me five times: he didn't protect me.

The taillight is out. Pull 'em over and put him in a body bag!

Save the Black man from police brutality and the body bags.

YEAR | 2016

WHAT HE WAS DOING | Pulled over for a traffic stop

HOW HE WAS KILLED | Police dash cam video of the traffic stop shows a police officer shooting Castile seconds after he informed him that he had a legal firearm. Castile's girlfriend was also in the car along with her four-year-old daughter; she captured the aftermath on Facebook live.

ACTION TAKEN | The officer charged was acquitted of second-degree manslaughter. The city agreed to a $3M settlement with Castile's mother.

We still can't breathe
A knee is on our necks
Life left
57%
Food for the soul

Pray early and often!

> *Psalm 94:21 | The wicked band together against the righteous and condemn the innocent to death.*

BRIANNA TAYLOR

THE LORD IS MY SAVIOR, and in life He has brought me a long way.
I think about my family and my friends as I lay here dying in my hallway.

Bullets really burn, and I can't explain the pain.
Five bullet holes are just too many...I don't think I can sustain.

The cops don't feel my pain because they're the ones who shot me.
Thirty-four shell casings, five in me; I can't believe they shot me.

This world that we live in feels like a prison.
The police are choosing who lives or who dies, and that's not their decision.

Even though I became a police brutality victim, my name will live forever, and I'll shine bright like a prism.

They will say my name #BriannaTaylor

They will say my name #BriannaTaylor

YEAR | 2020

WHAT SHE WAS DOING | Asleep at home.

HOW SHE WAS KILLED | Taylor and her boyfriend were sleeping when three plainclothes officers arrived at their apartment to execute a search warrant in a drug case. Taylor's boyfriend called 911 and fired his licensed firearm. Taylor, who was unarmed, was shot five times.

We still can't breathe
A knee is on our necks
Life left
50%
Food for the soul

To have faith is to keep faith.

> *Leviticus 24:19-20 | Anyone who injures their neighbor is to be injured in the same manner: fracture for fracture, eye for an eye, tooth for a tooth. The one who has inflicted the injury must suffer the same injury.*

EMMETT TILL

I WAS ONLY fourteen years old when I was lynched in Mississippi in 1955, after being accused of offending a white woman in her family's grocery store. The two white men who murdered me made me unwillingly carry a seventy-five-pound cotton-gin fan to the bank of the Tallahatchie River and ordered me to take off my clothes.

The two white men nearly beat me to death.

They gouged out my eyes, shot me in the head, and threw my body (tied to a cotton-gin fan with barbed wire) into the river.

In September of 1955, an all-white jury found the two white men not guilty of kidnapping and murdering me.

Protected against double jeopardy, the two white men publicly admitted in a 1956 interview with Look Magazine that they had kidnapped and murdered me.

I still can't breathe!

DO YOU REMEMBER?

Do you remember how I was kidnapped, and murdered by those two white men who later proudly admitted to kidnapping and murdering me? I'll never forget!

We still can't breathe
A knee is on our necks
Life left
46%
Food for the soul

#SaveTheBlackMan

Galatians 5:14 | For all the law is fulfilled in one word, even in this: you shall love your neighbor as yourself.

MEDGAR EVERS

ON JUNE 12TH, 1963, Mississippi was divided by racism and hate. At thirty-seven years old I was assassinated by a white supremacist.

I was shot and killed by a high powered rifle. Serving my country as a World War II veteran, I honestly believed that my life would end differently after everything I fought for.

I was fighting for change. I was fighting for equality. I fought against police brutality, racism, and hate.

This country has been divided since the beginning of time. Hate overpowers love in America, but as a whole we have the power to tip the scale. Choose love over hate and don't fight fire with fire. Let's work together and help each other breathe as long as there's breath in our bodies.

DO YOU REMEMBER?

Do you remember how I was gunned down by the hands of a white supremacist? I was shot and killed with a high powered rifle right in my driveway. I'll never forget!

We still can't breathe
A knee is on our necks
Life left
39%
Food for the soul

Strengthen our youth, mentally. Help to inspire the next generation.

> *Deuteronomy 10:17 | For the Lord your God is God of Gods and Lord of Lords, the great God, mighty, awesome, who shows no partiality nor takes a bribe.*

Rosa Parks

ON DECEMBER 1ST, 1955, I was forty-two years old when I was arrested in Montgomery, Alabama for refusing to give up my seat on a public bus. The white section of the segregated bus was filled, and therefore a white passenger was legally entitled to sit down and make me stand.

Segregation was written into law: the front of the Montgomery bus was reserved for white citizens, and the seats behind them for Black citizens. However, it was only by custom that bus drivers had the authority to ask a Black person to give up their seat for a white rider, and they were sometimes forced to stand to add more room for white riders.

On December 1st, 1955, I was tired. I felt like I couldn't breathe...but I wasn't tired, physically. I was tired of giving in, so I sat in the front of the bus for equality.

DO YOU REMEMBER?

Do you remember that there was a time when Blacks were forced to sit in the back of the bus—or stand—to make room for white riders? I'll never forget!

We still can't breathe
A knee is on our necks
Life left
31%
Food for the soul

Educate yourself on Black history and understand how hard our ancestors fought for us to be where we are today.

John 13:34 | A new command I give you: love one another. As I have loved you, so you must love one another.

MILLION MAN MARCH

I CAN FEEL it in my soul, and I can feel it in my heart.
That the time is now for us to have another Million Man
March.

400 years later, and the pain is still severe.
Kneeling for the flag is not enough; they still can't see us, or
hear.

They have something to fear, and that's all Blacks coming
together.
The day that we finally choose to stand and move as one will
be stronger than whoever.

Together we shall stand and fight for what we believe in!
This will bring less pain, less heartache, and less grieving.

Unity and family values, that's what we protect.
Just because the shade of our skin is darker, we still want our
respect.
The same respect everyone deserves because respect is
earned and achieved.
We don't want to feel like a knee is on our necks, and that it's
hard for us to breathe.

DO YOU REMEMBER?

Do you remember when over a million Black men came together for atonement and reconciliation? I'll never forget!

We still can't breathe
A knee is on our necks
Life left
27%
Food for the soul

Don't wait for change. Be the change.

Romans 1:28-29 | And even as they did not like to retain God in their knowledge, God gave them over to a reprobate mind, to do those which are not convenient; being filled with all unrighteousness, fortification, wickedness, covetousness, maliciousness; full of envy, murder, debate, deceit, malignity; whispers.

KUNTA KINTE

I'M FROM THE African village of Juffure, and this beautiful place still exists.

400 years ago, white men came to our land with their guns and their ships.

The white men put us in shackles and chains and then beat us with whips.

Then the white men unknowingly took us to America and cotton was picked.

Slave catchers gave me a choice to be castrated, or to chop off my foot.

I just wanted to taste freedom, but they crippled me when they chopped off my foot.

The white men raped our women and abused our children.

400 years later, go to any old slave camp and the spirits...you still feel them.

I am a Mandinka warrior. My name is Kunta Kinte, not Toby.

I am Black, proud, and powerful. You know me.

We are the chosen people and the white man stole us from our land.

My name is Kunta Kinte. I'll never forget who I am.

DO YOU REMEMBER?

Do you remember how the white man stole us from our land only to bring us to an unknown land to slave and work for free? I'll never forget!

We still can't breathe
A knee is on our necks
Life left
20%
Food for the soul

Connect with your roots!

Isaiah 40:31 | But those that wait upon the Lord shall renew their strength; they shall mount up with wings as eagles; they shall run, and not be weary; and they shall walk, and not faint.

Harriet Tubman

CAN YOU IMAGINE having a two-pound weight violently thrown at your head?
That's what a slave master did to me, and I endured seizures, severe headaches, and narcoleptic episodes for years.

I remember one morning before breakfast, a slave master whipped me five times...and I still carry those scars. I knew that in that moment it was time for a change, and it was time to go far.

I was born into slavery, but my spirit allowed me to see more. The Underground Railroad gave me purpose, self-value, and room to restore.

In 1849, I finally escaped to freedom. Through the Underground Railroad, my purpose led me back to free hundreds of people.

In 2016, I was acknowledged highly, and now they want to put my face on a $20 bill.

All I ever wanted was for Blacks to be free and treated equal, and that's real.

I just want us to breathe again. Let us be free!

Free yourselves from those chains: physically, and mentally.

DO YOU REMEMBER?

Do you remember that I was born a slave? Do you remember that I escaped slavery and became free? Do you remember how I came back for other slaves so that they could also be free? I'll never forget!

We still can't breathe
A knee is on our necks
Life left
13%
Food for the soul

Reveal the purpose within you!

> *Ephesians 2:14 | For he himself is our peace, who has made two groups one and has destroyed the barrier, the dividing wall of hostility.*

Martin Luther King Jr.

BLACK MEN ARE still languishing in corners of American society, and we find ourselves being exiled in our own land. We've come here today to dramatize a shameful condition. In a sense, we've come to our nation's capital to cash a check. When the architects of our republic wrote the magnificent words of the Constitution and Declaration of Independence, they were signing a promissory note to which every American was to fall heir. This note was a promise that all men—yes, Black men as well as white men—would be guaranteed the unalienable rights of life, liberty, and the pursuit of happiness. It is obvious today that America has defaulted on this promissory note insofar as her citizens of color are concerned. Instead of honoring this sacred obligation, America has given Black people a bad check, a check which has come back marked insufficient funds.

DO YOU REMEMBER?

Do you remember that I had a dream? I'll never forget!

We still can't breathe
A knee is on our necks
Life left
2%
Food for the soul

Use your voice!

> *John 14:20 | On that day you will know that I am in my father, and you in me, and I in you.*

EPILOGUE

THE FIRST THING I'll say is that Black is beautiful. How can you not notice that with your eyes? Black is brilliant. How can you not believe that in your heart?

Black has been here from the start. You cannot depart what is.

I am. You cannot tell me that I'm not, because I know, and I understand.

Unity and love will overpower hate. It just takes time. Set your watch and wait. You will see in future times.

I love you all and you don't have to say it back. I took my time to write these words for us, praying we will stay on track. I want us back.

Let us breathe again!

NEVER FORGET

Never forget about the people who are still mourning from their lost loved ones becoming victims of police brutality. Never forget that justice still hasn't prevailed in many of those police brutality cases. Never forget about the racism, hate, and pain that our ancestors went through. Never forget how hard they fought to change our circumstances. Never forget why we are where we are today. I'll never forget!

We still can't breathe
A knee is on our necks
Life left
0%
Food for the soul

Believe in yourself.

I Still Can't Breathe 400 Years Later

www.ingramcontent.com/pod-product-compliance
Lightning Source LLC
Chambersburg PA
CBHW011232120626
46549CB00008B/3244